Adult Coloring Book
Auntie V.'s
Mandalas

By: V. Pereira

Adult Coloring Book
Auntie V.'s
Mandalas

ISBN-13:978-1530239863

ISBN-10:1530239869

Mandalas often contain visual elements

that are balanced to remind us to stay

harmonious on our spiritual journeys.

Close your eyes and relax for a few minutes

before starting your mandala.

Remember to be thankful and positive as

you color your way to a calmer, happier you!

Life is too short to be anything but happy

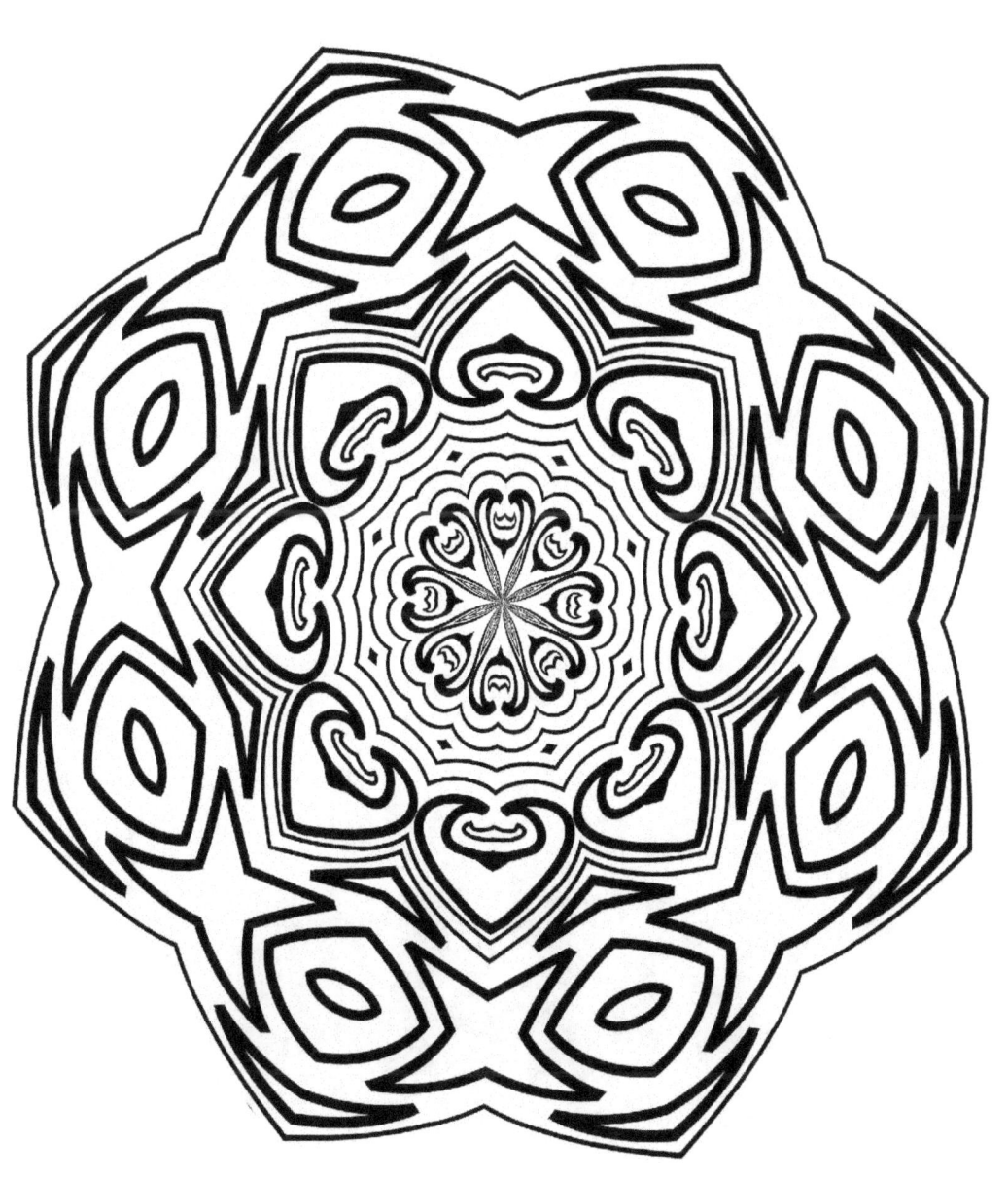

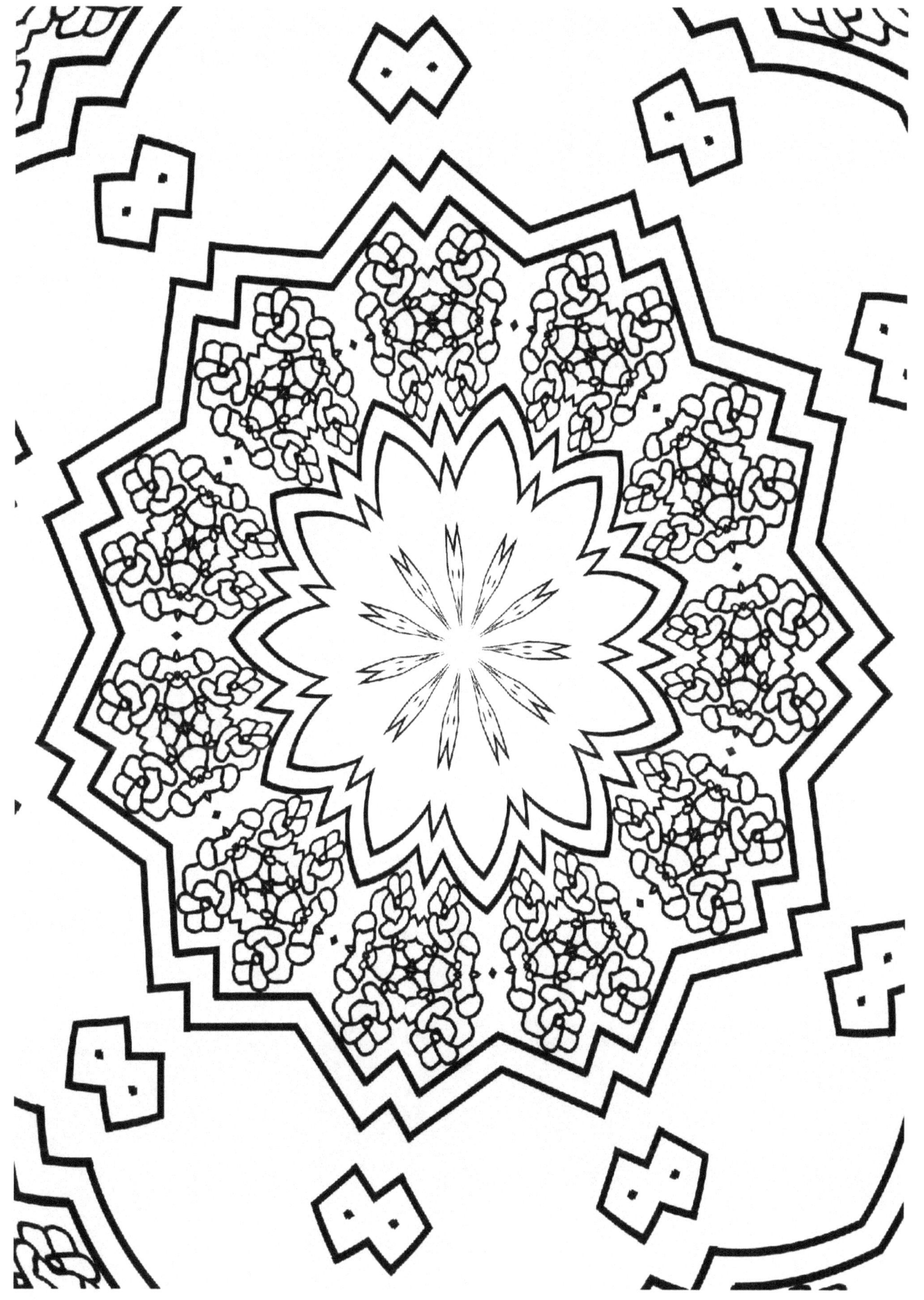

I'm in the right place,
doing the right thing,
at the right time.

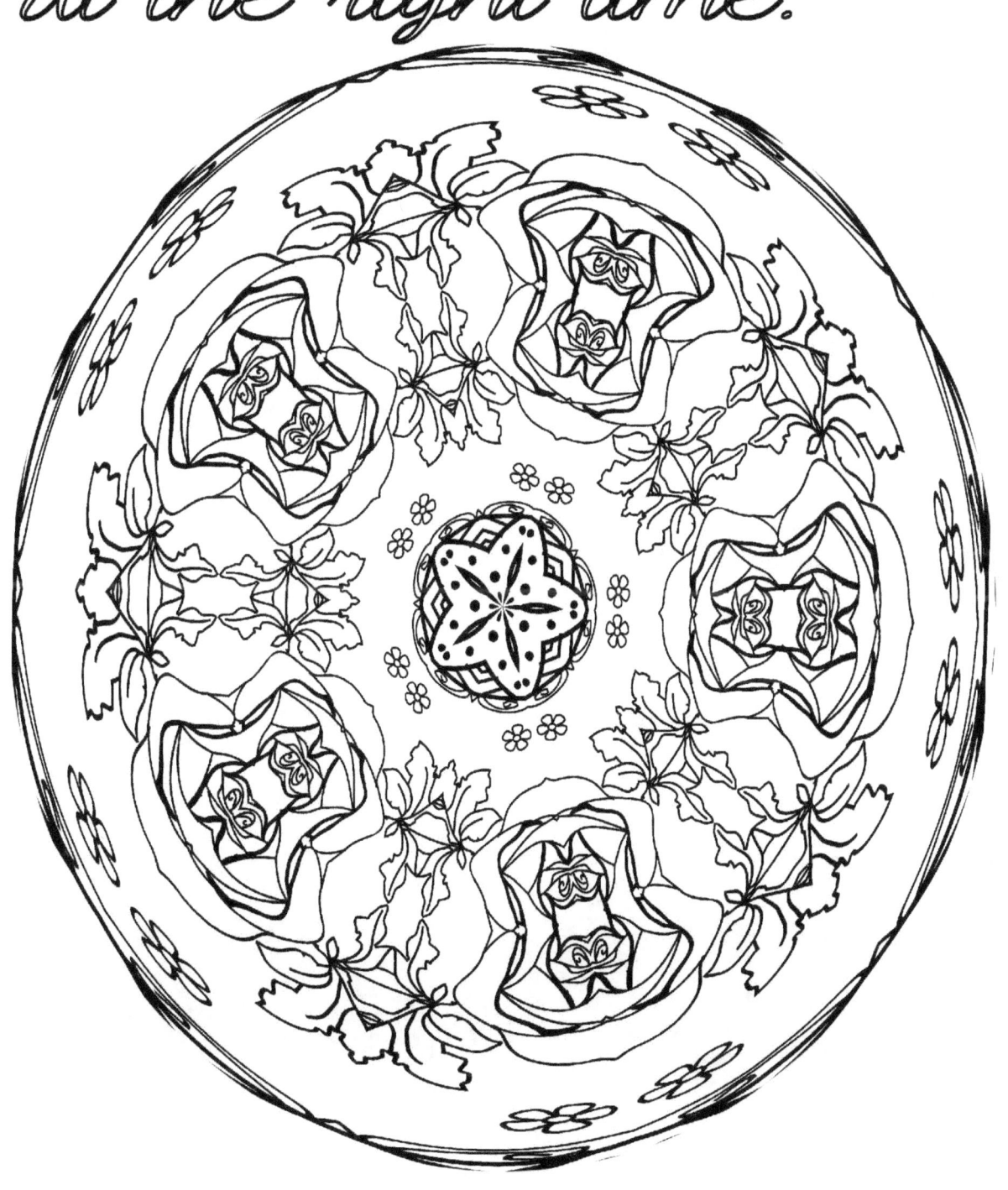

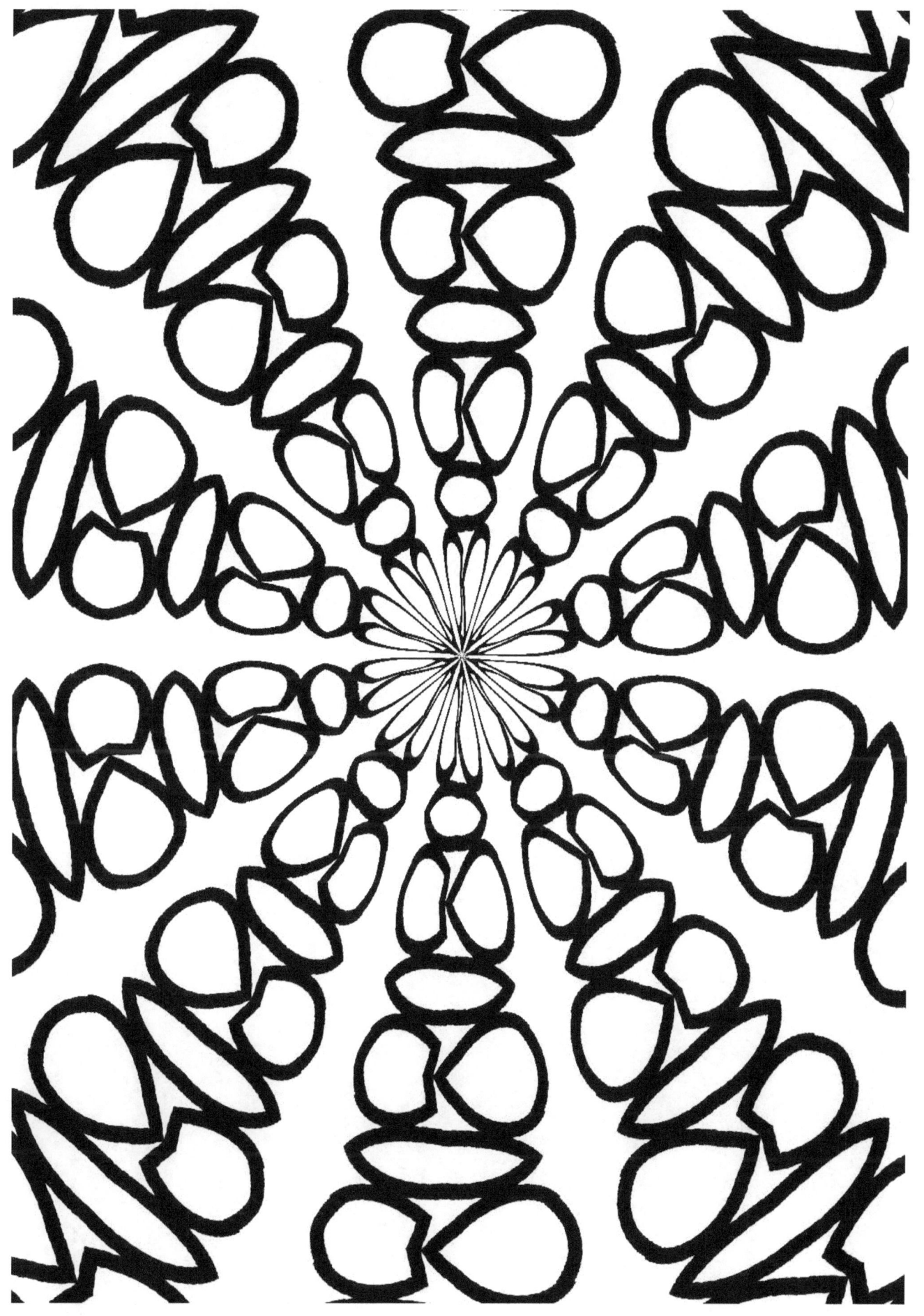

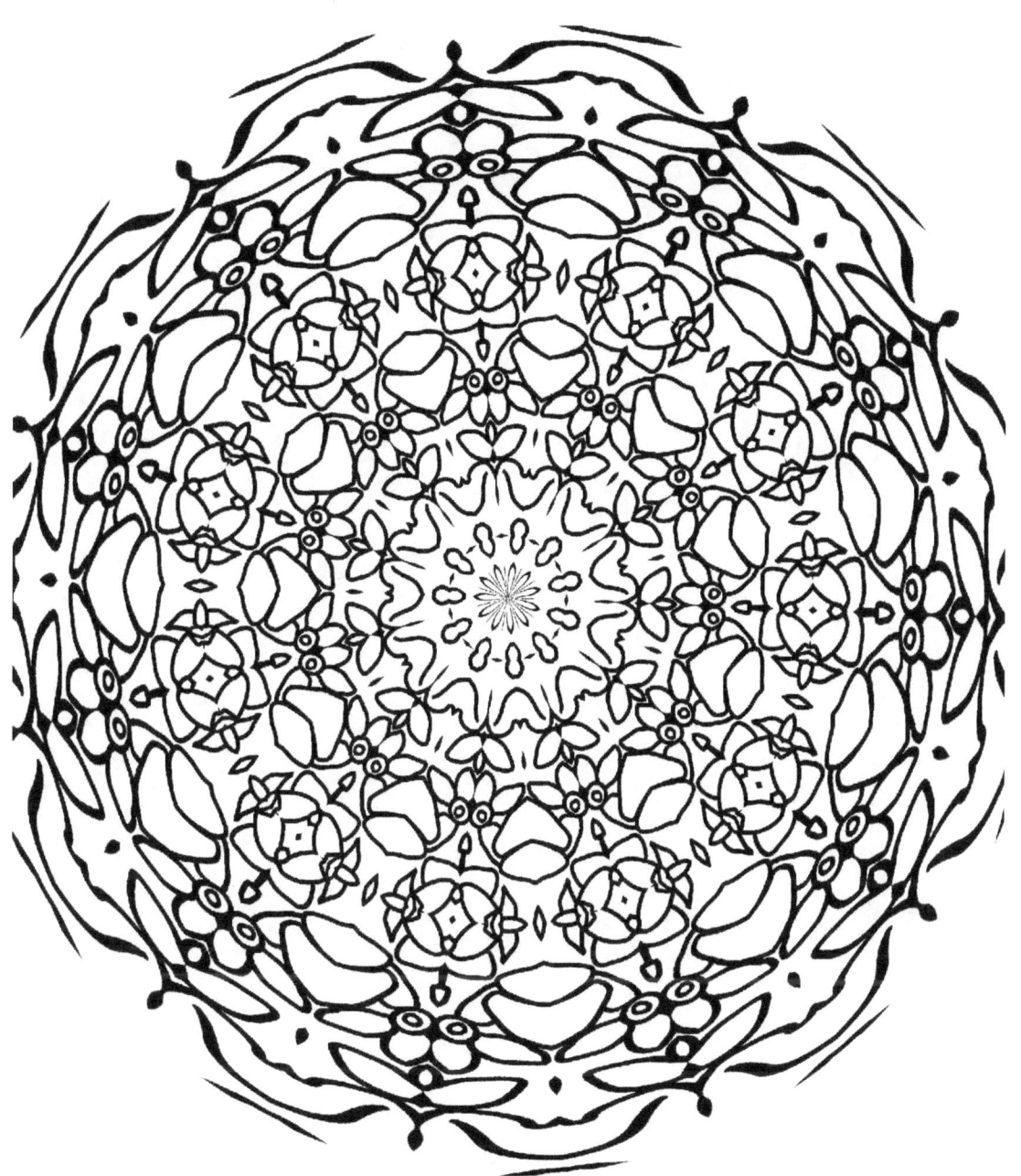

I AM ALIGNED

With the energy of

Abundance

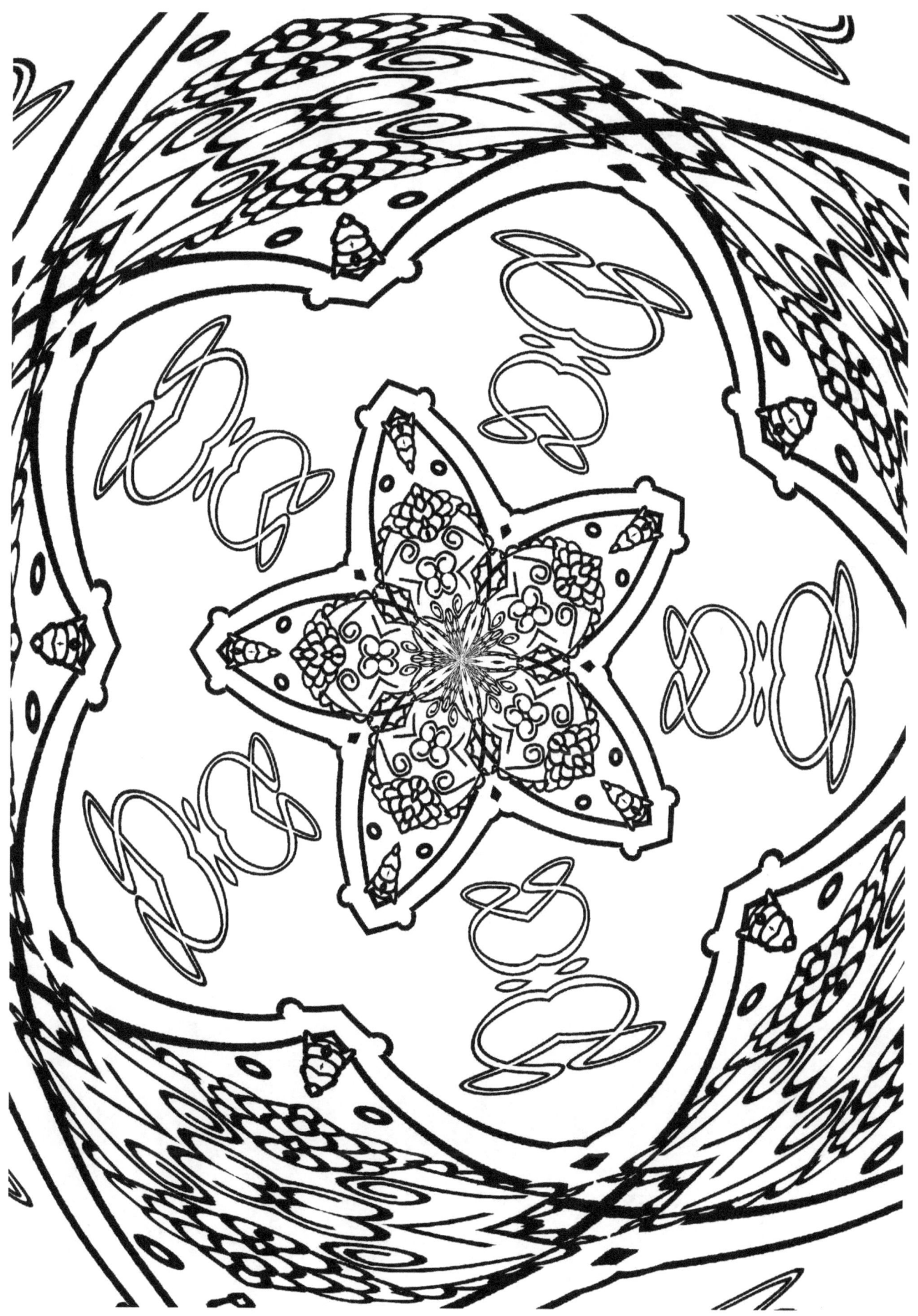

I have a vast and wondrous

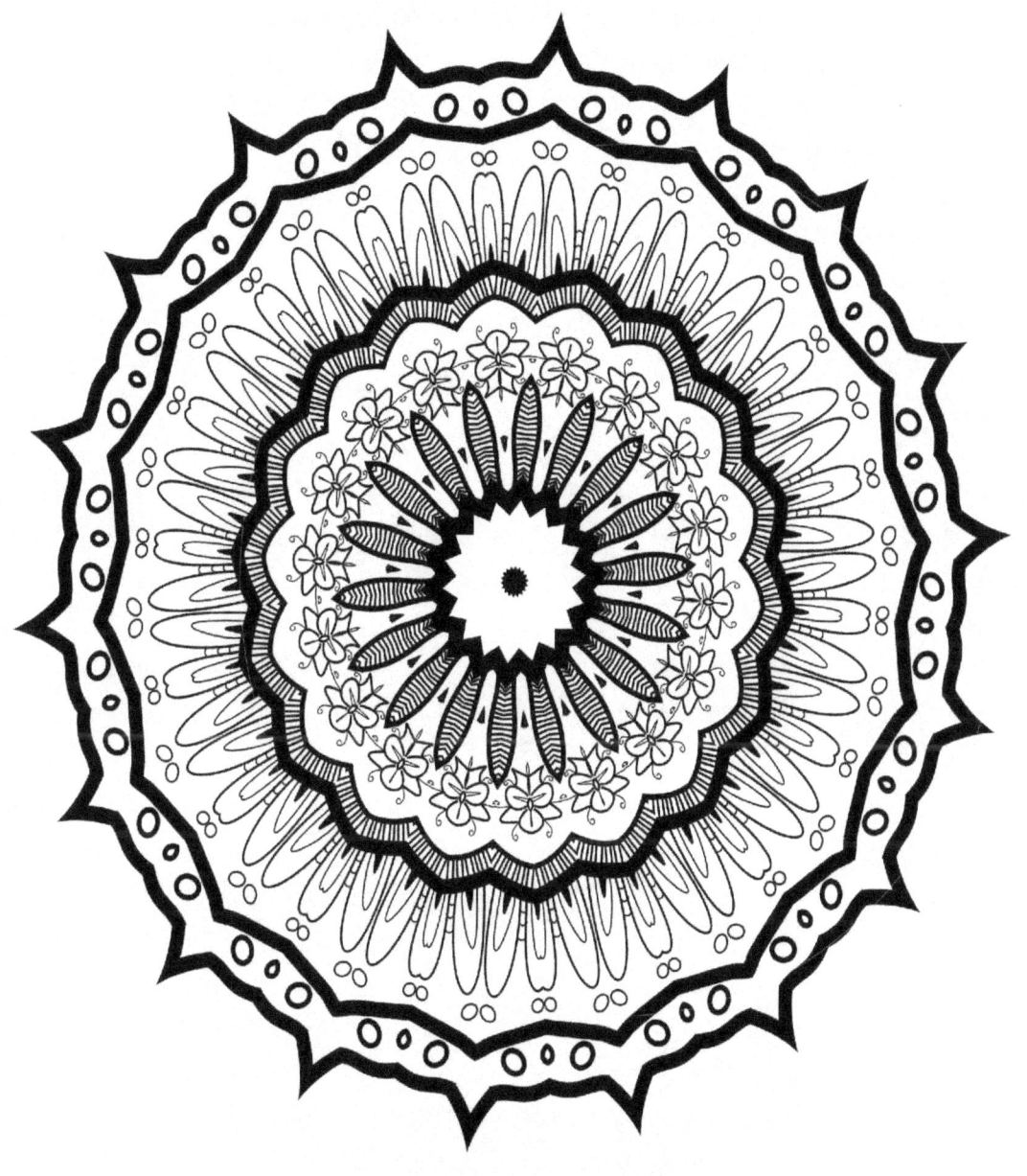

IMAGINATION

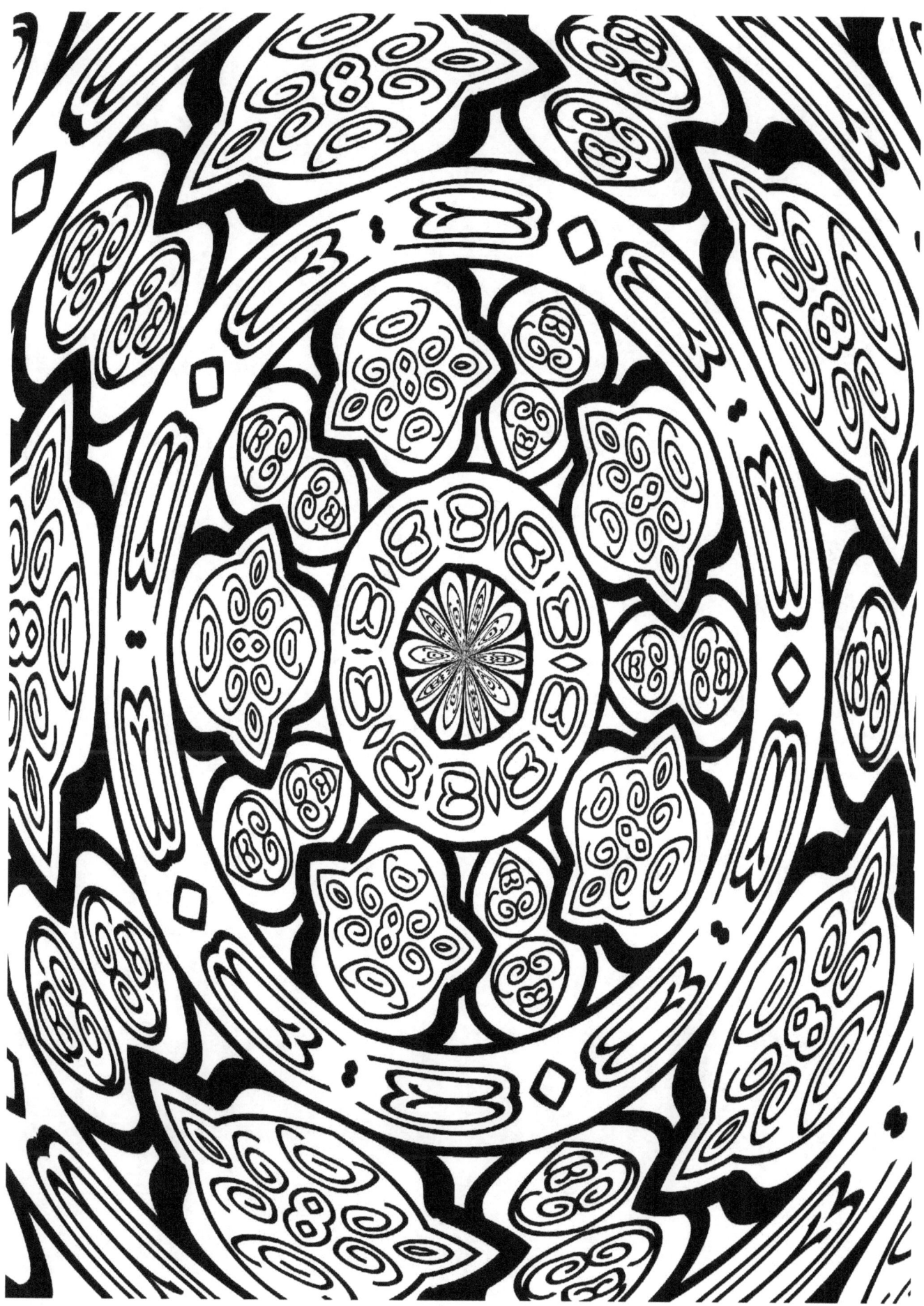

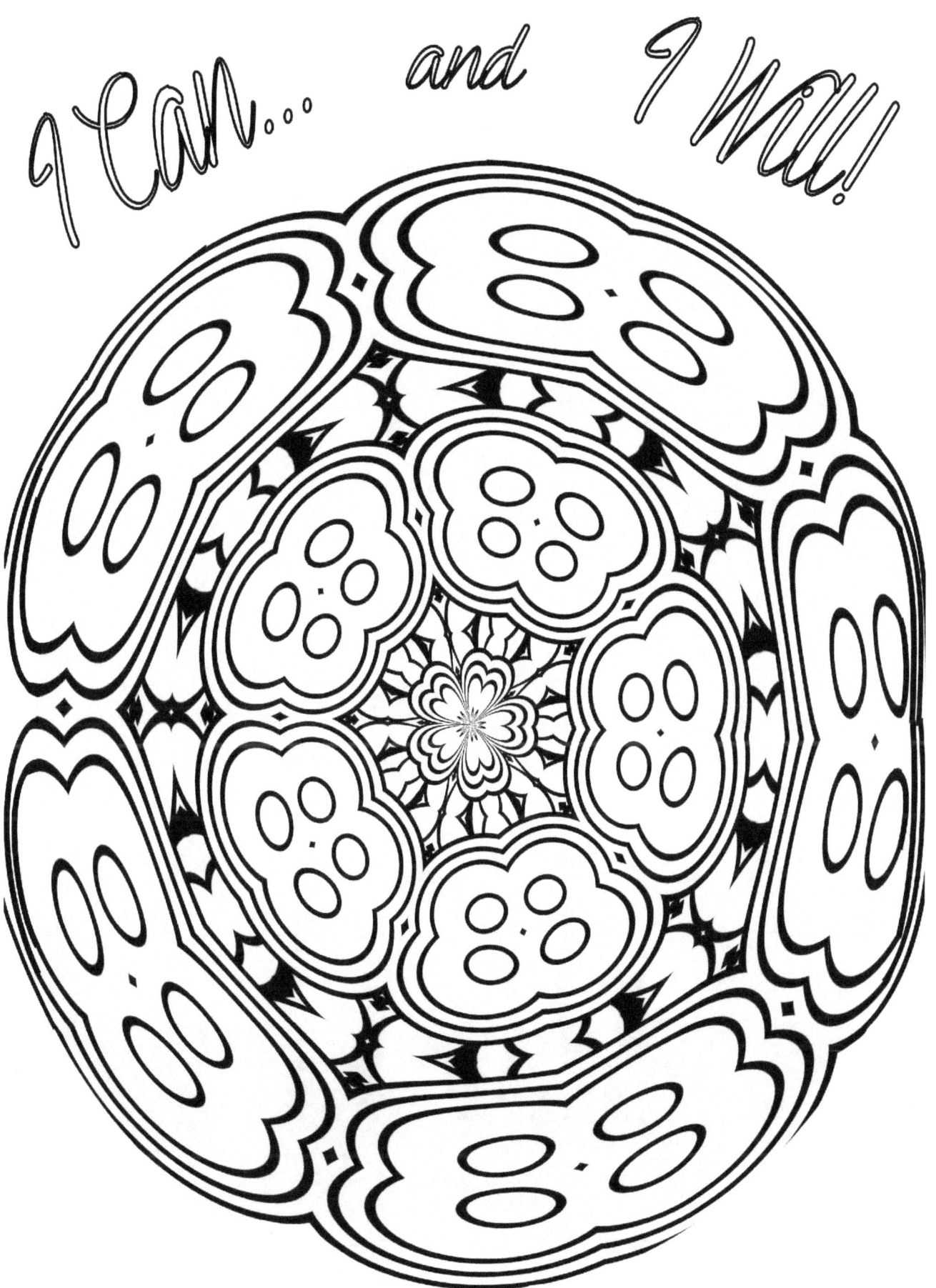

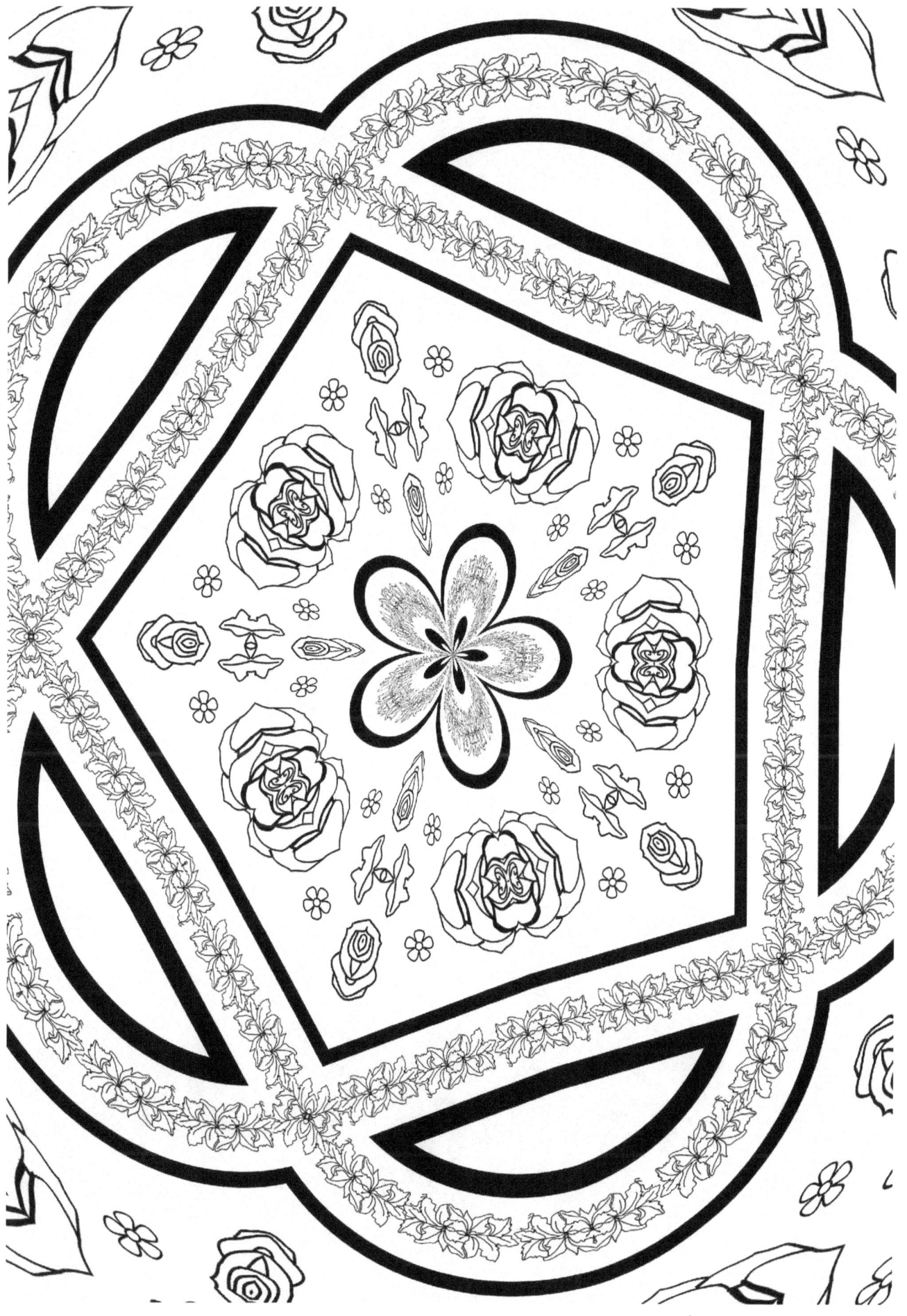

Today

I believe in Myself...

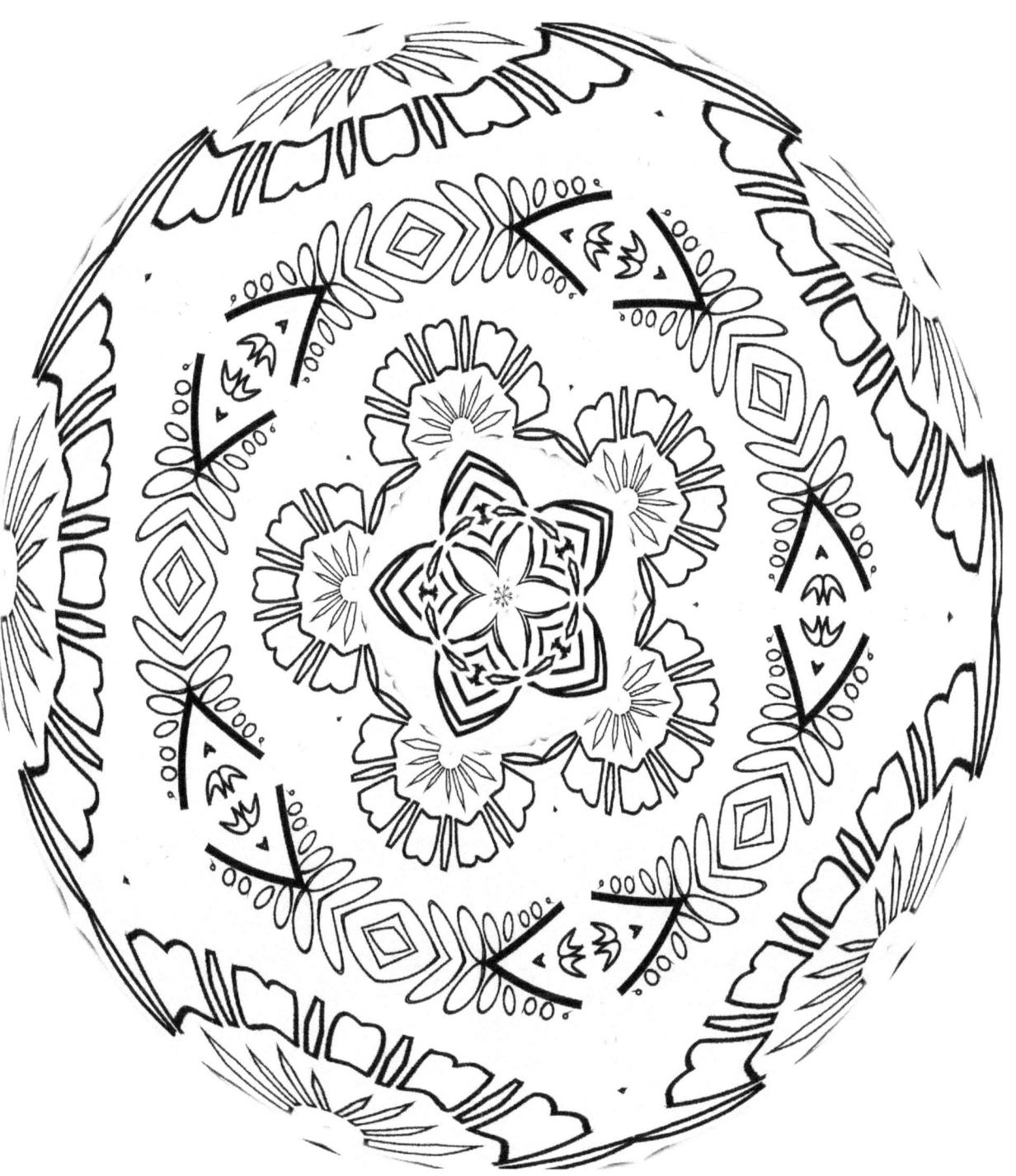

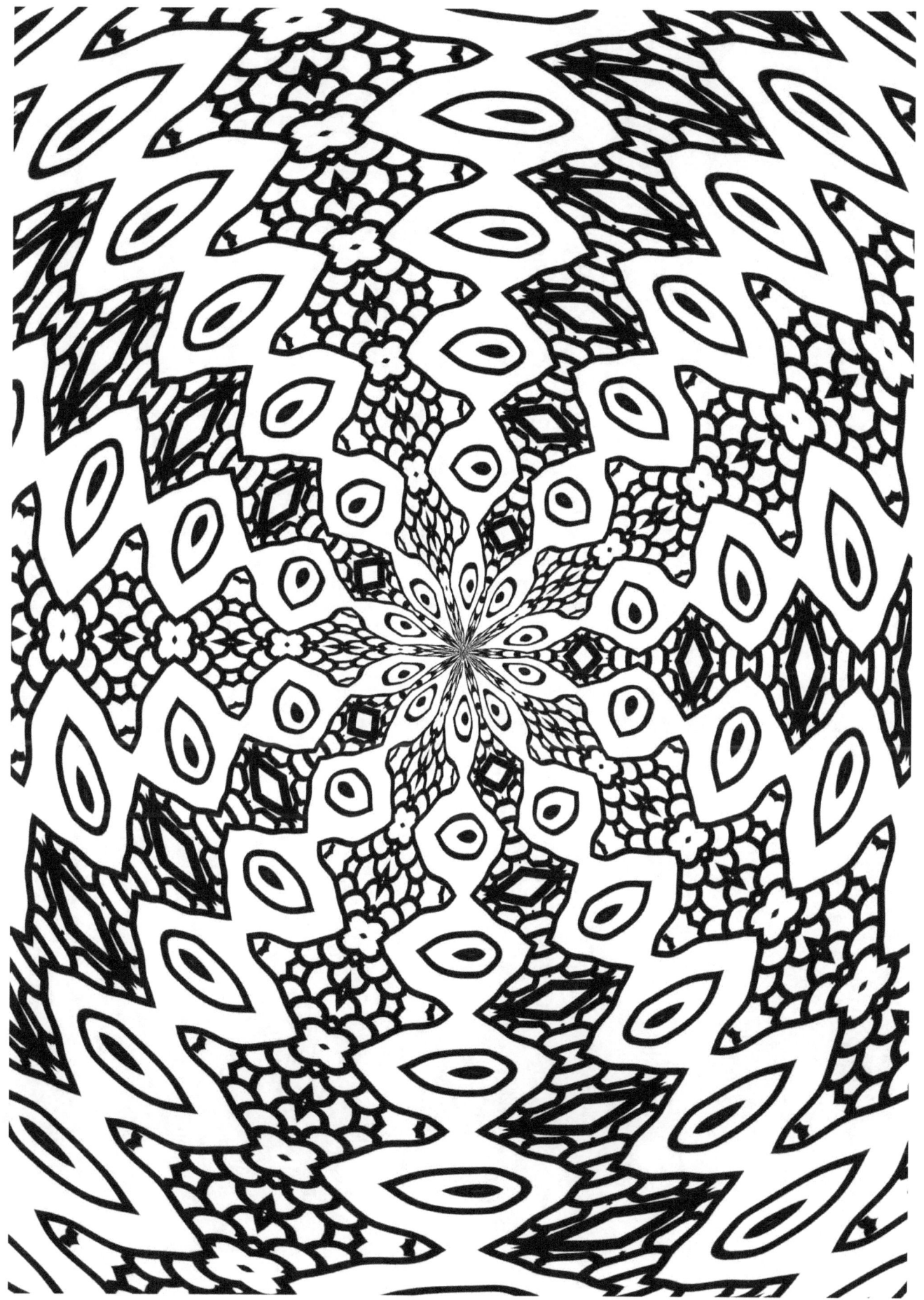

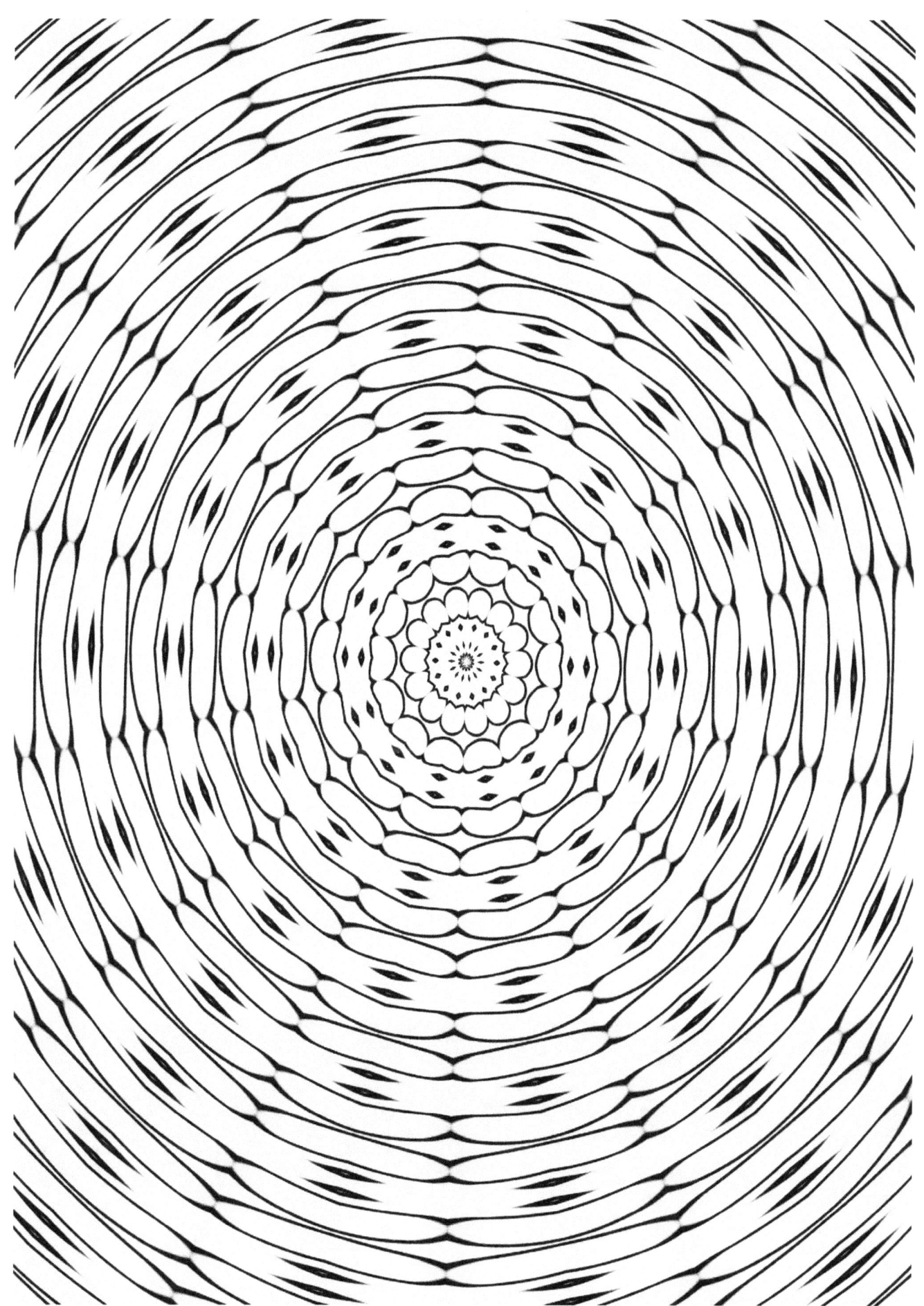

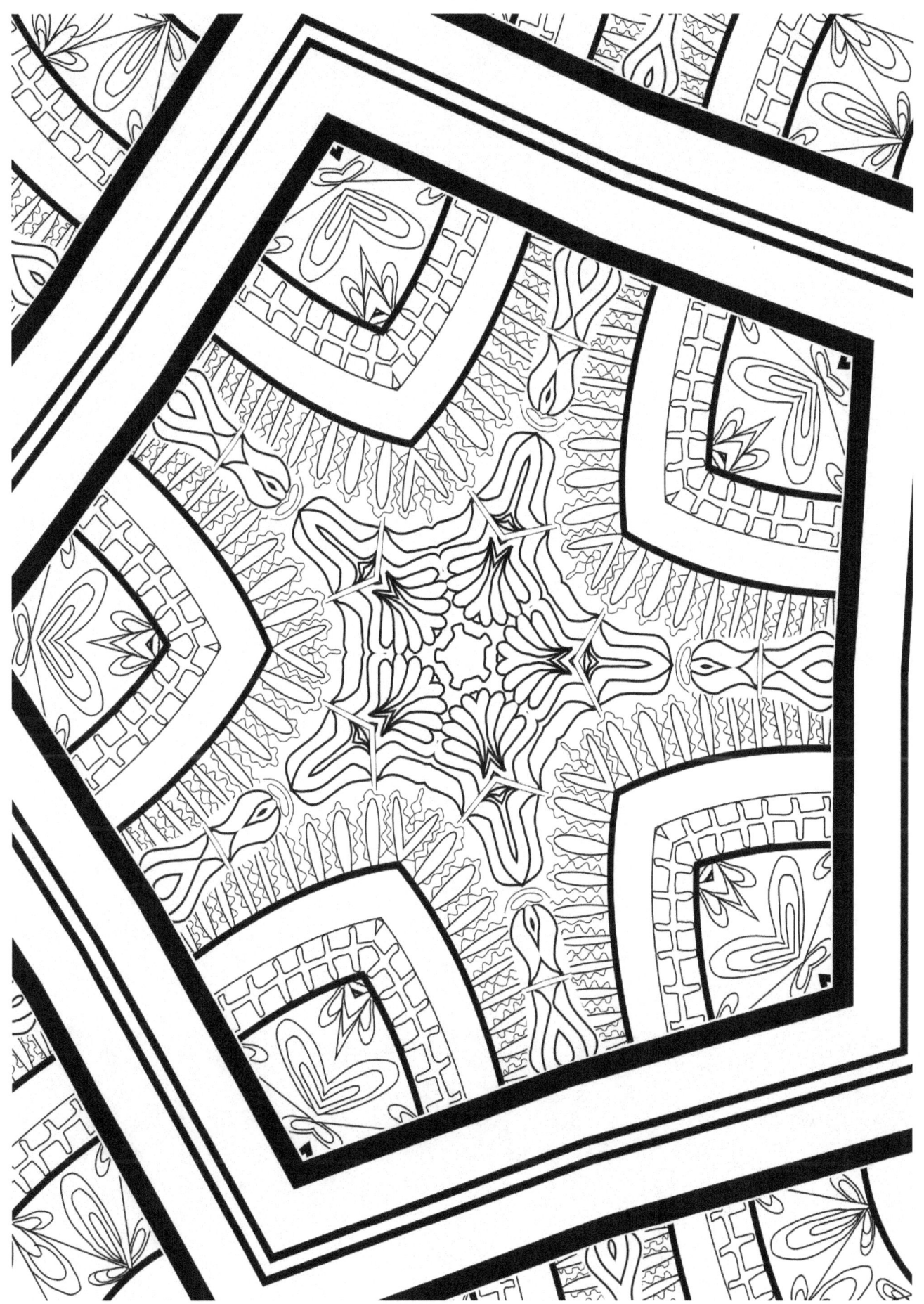

She turned her
'can'ts' into 'cans'
and her dreams into PLANS

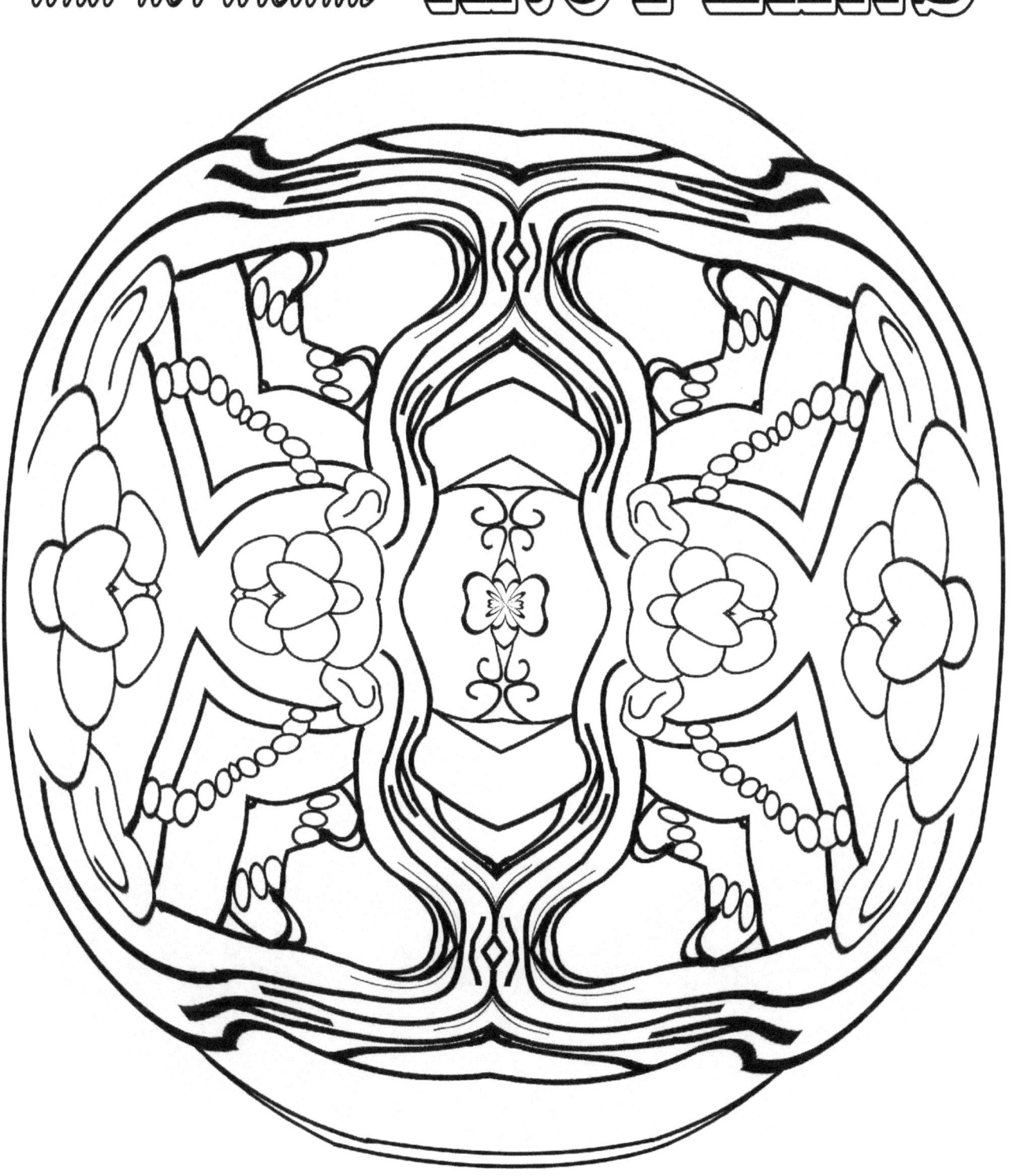

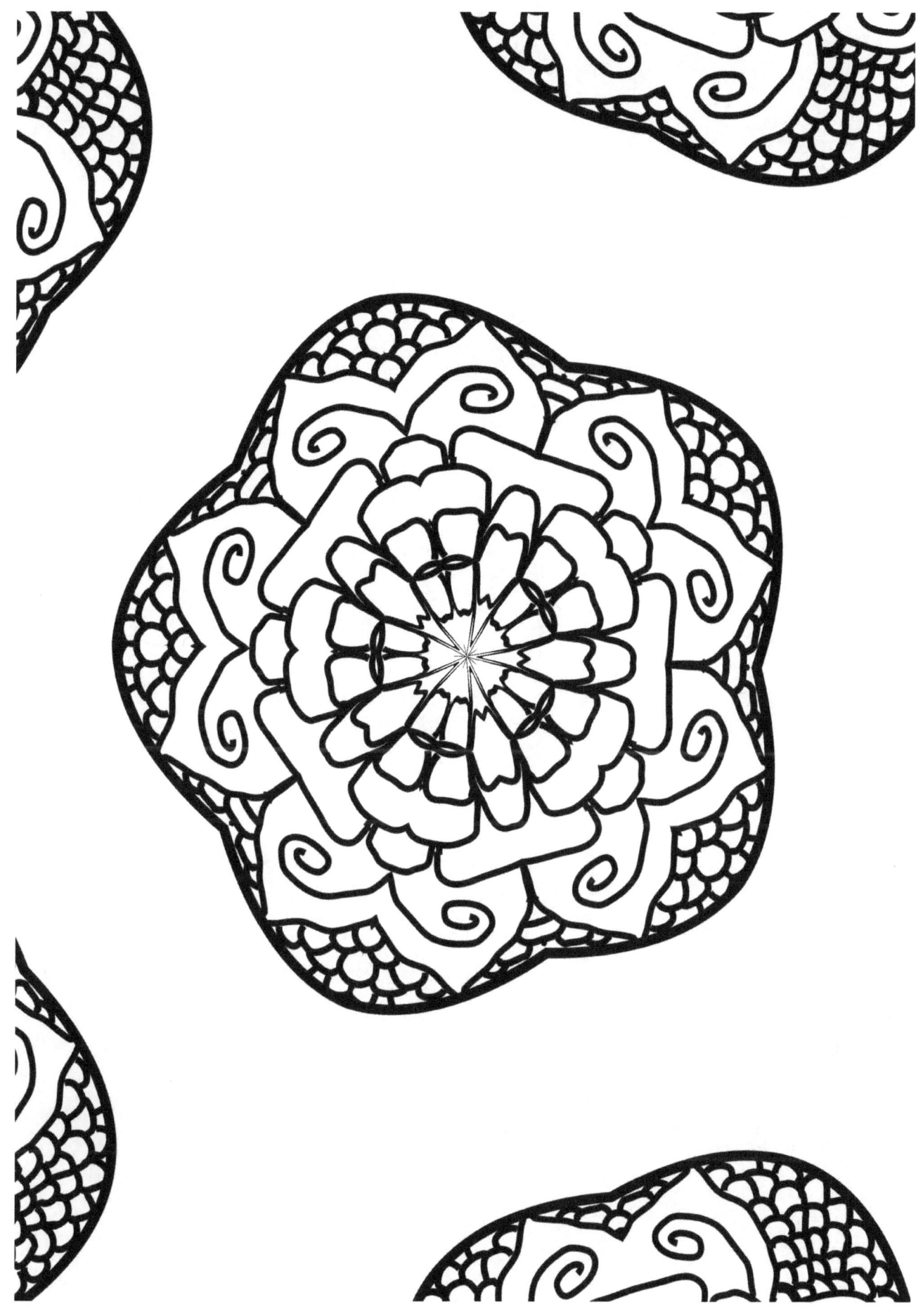

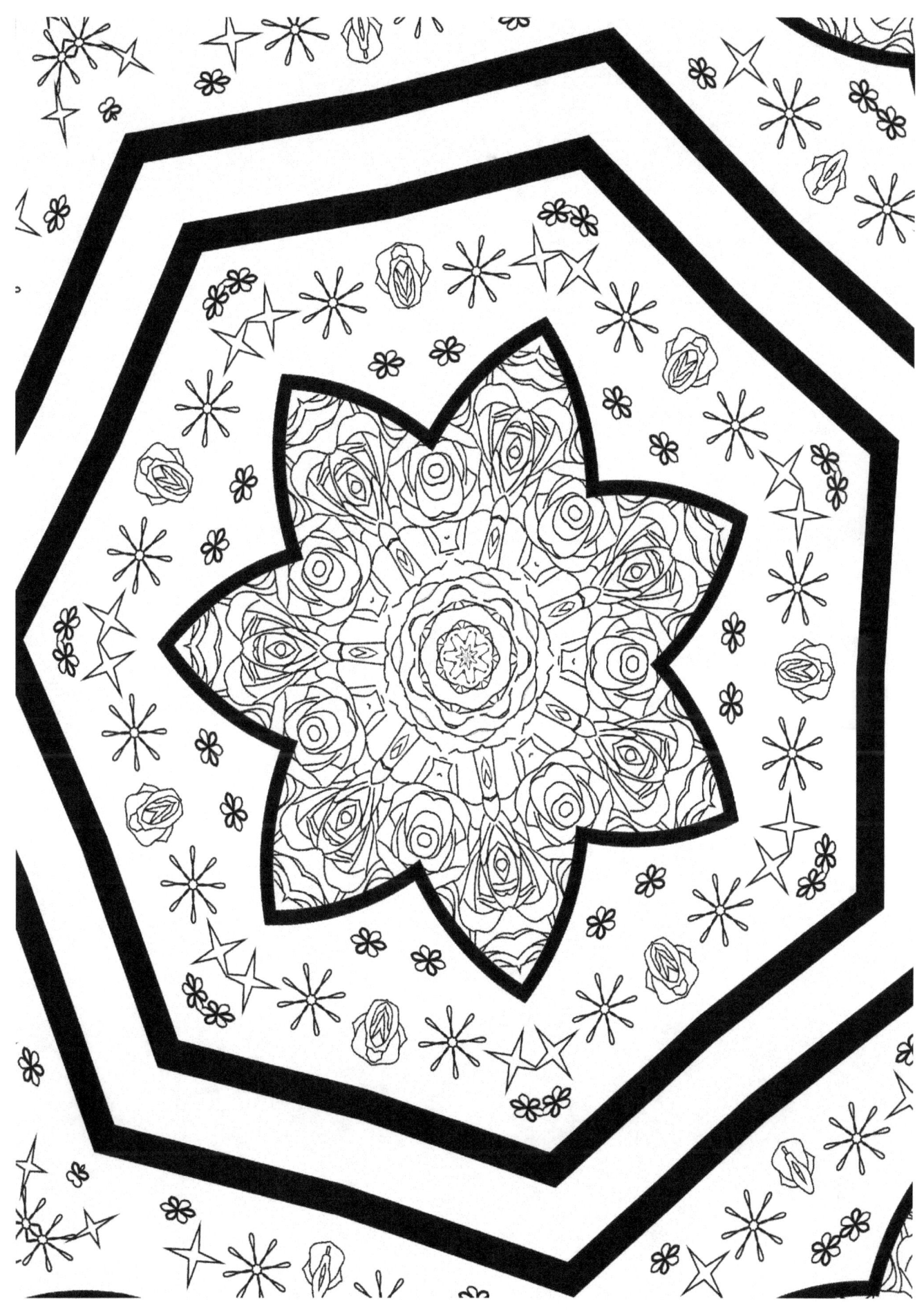

The Universe

Provides me with All
That I will ever need.

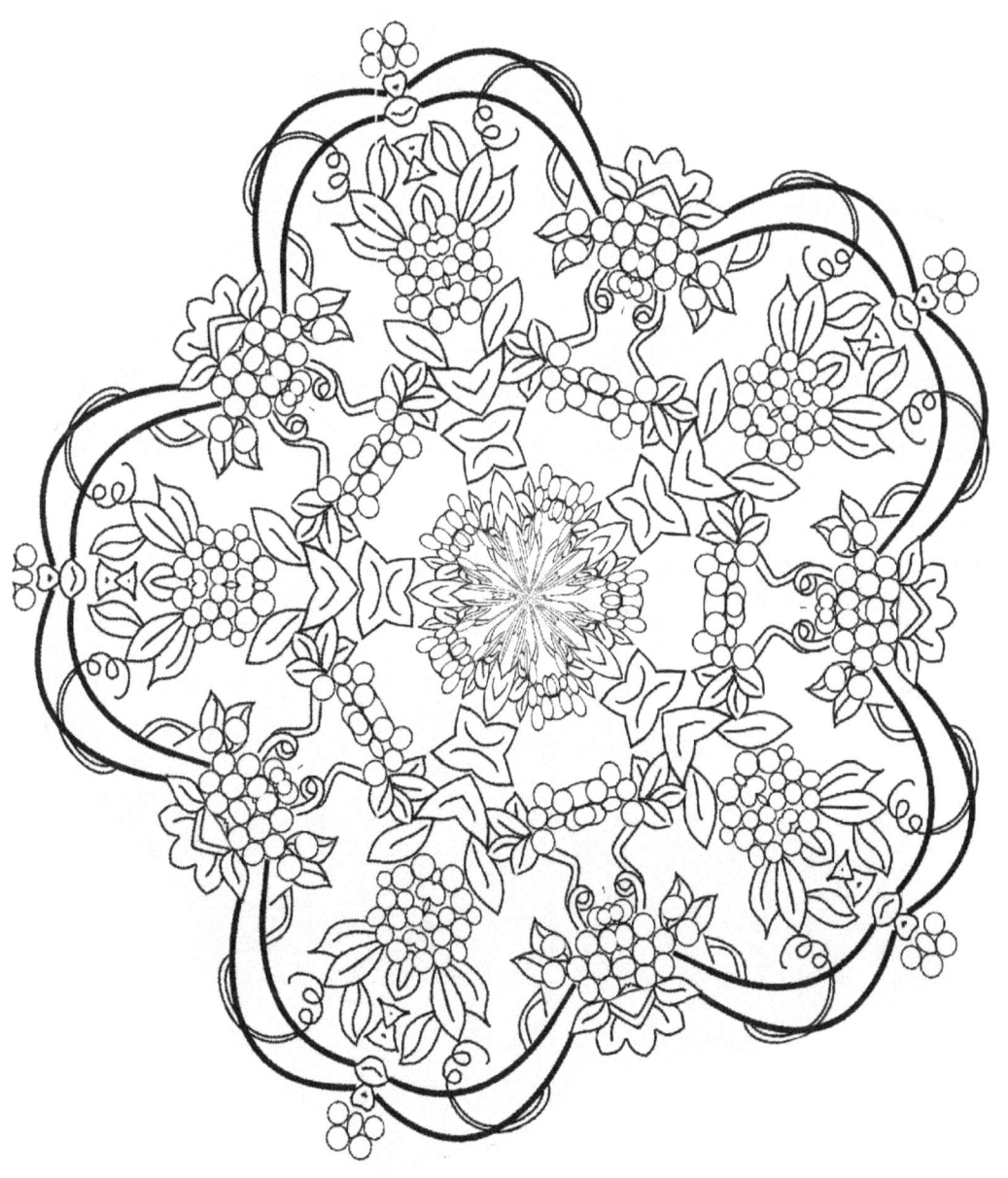

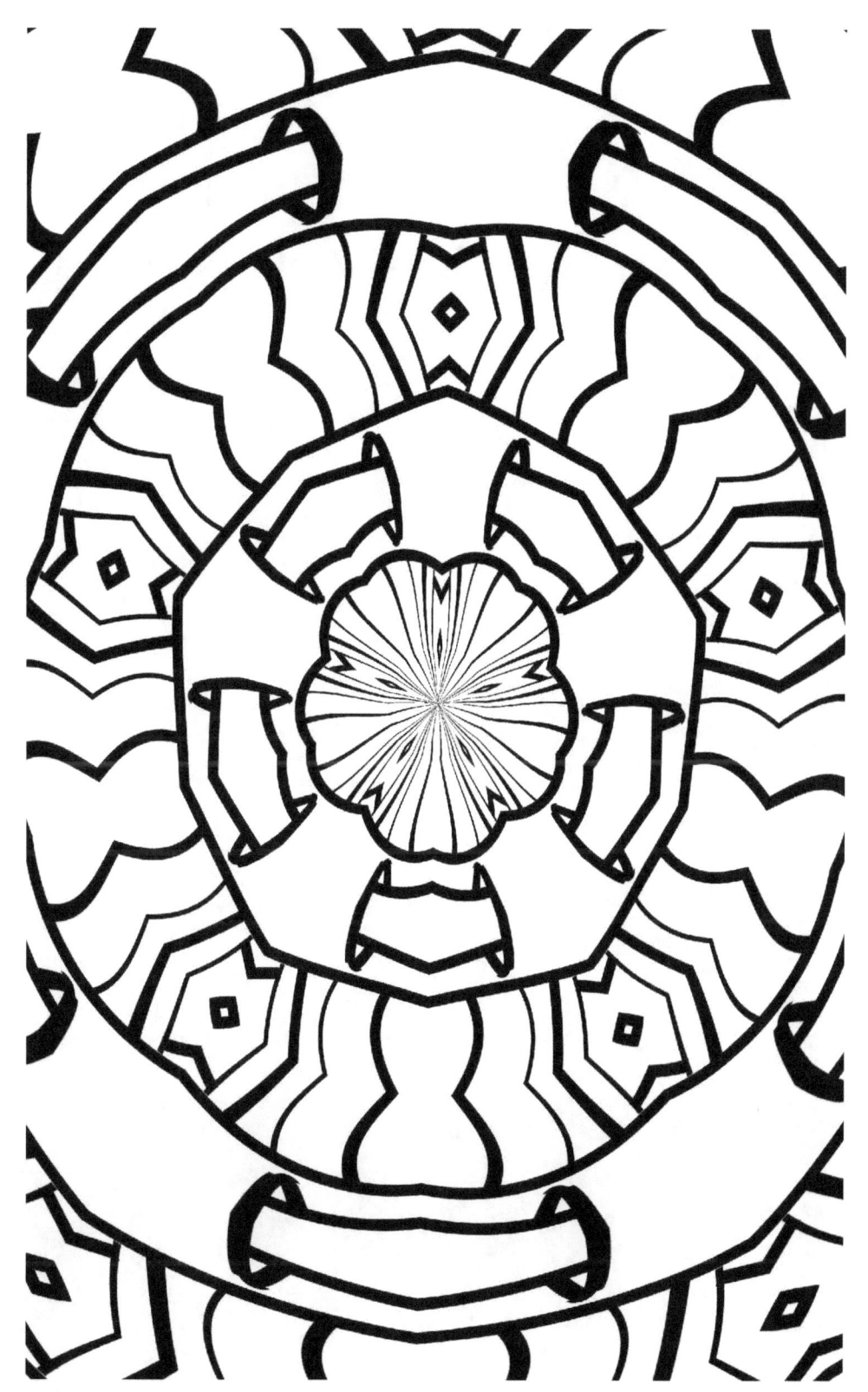

I Breath in Peace...
I Breath out Peace...

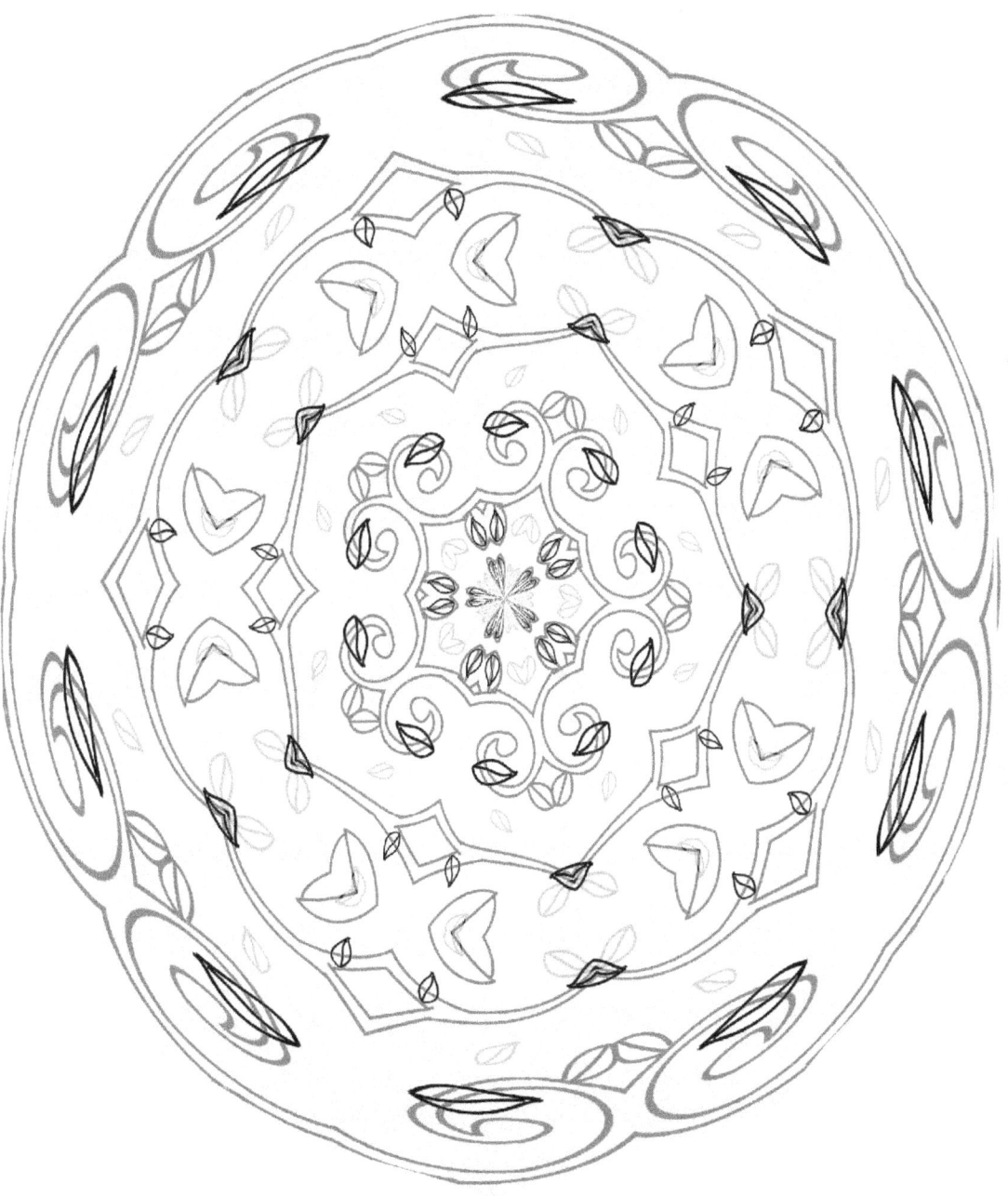

I AM Peace!

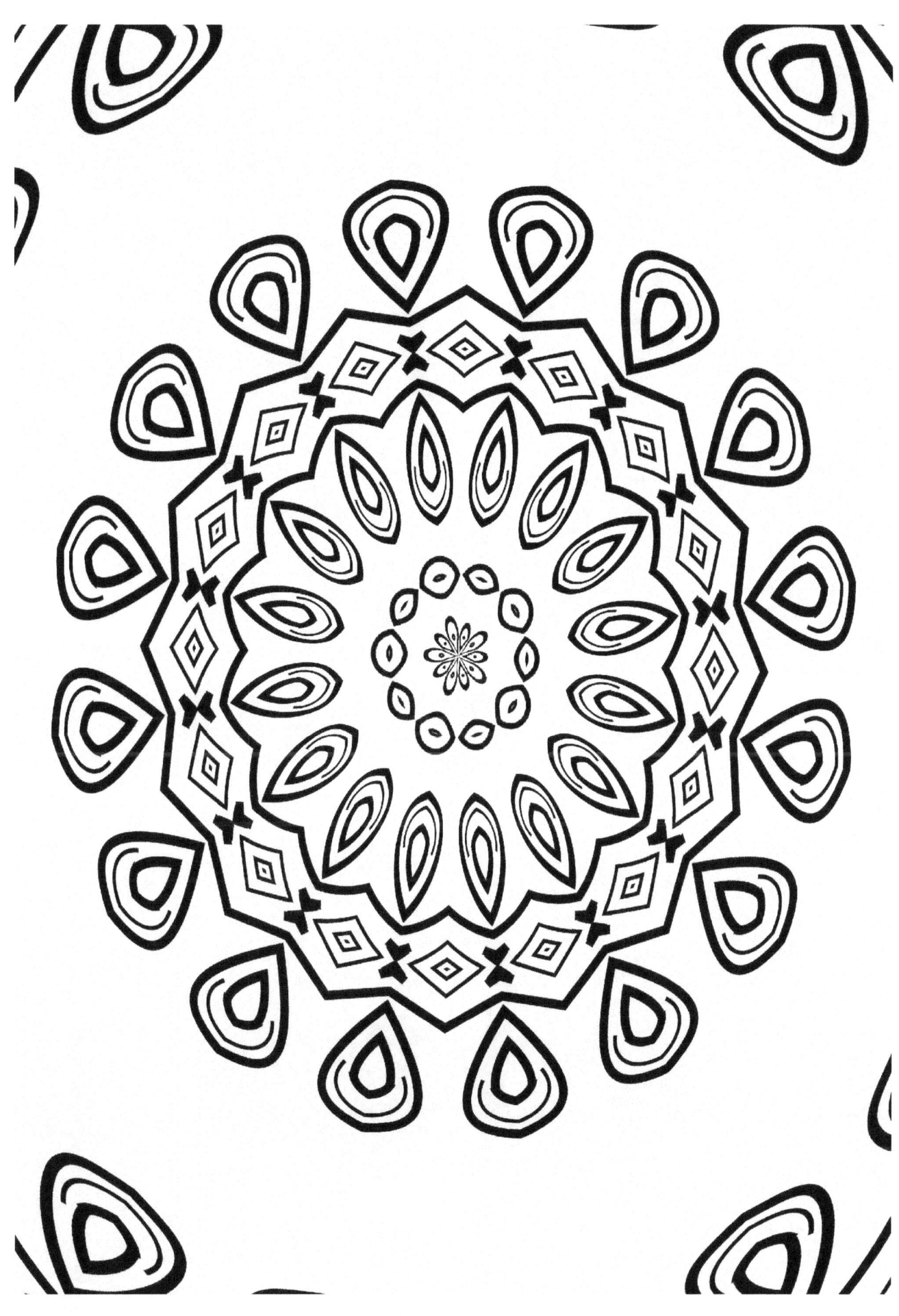

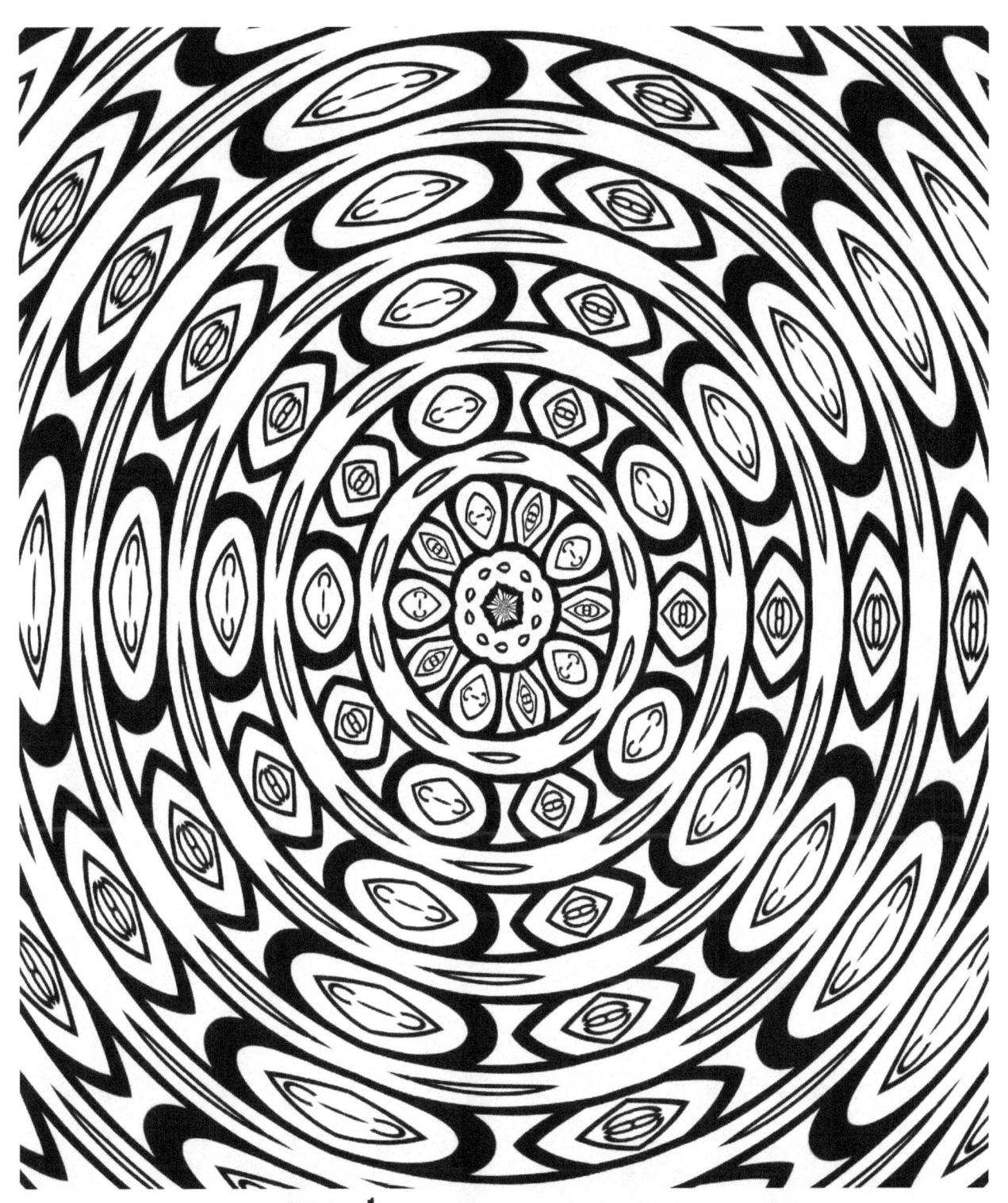

I Now Free Myself
From Destructive
Fears and Doubts